*   *

"These poems, almost hallucinogenic in their intensity, present an embodied experience - the thinking mind must catch up when it can. The language is rich and visceral - every word has weight."
— Patrick Cosgrove, VSO Tanzania 1996-98.

*   *   *

"Red Winds is an account of Irma Upex-Huggins' time with the VSO in Tanzania, living and working in an environment of extreme poverty, and it charts her journey through the country and through illness and recovery from a serious accident. Red Winds is a combination of poetry and prose, letters from Africa.

Irma was born in Antigua in the West Indies, finished school in Nevis and came to live in England. But as a black woman now coming from England to Tanzania she has a sense of dislocation, 'an uncomfortable sense of my 'not-belonging': when I feel that my 'Africanness' is still wandering in the Diaspora', when asked 'Kabila Gani?', meaning what is your Tribe, her reply is 'Sina'- I have none. She is marked as an Outsider by her lack of Swahili, and even by her hair, worn in a style of Maasai men.

Irma is called 'Mzungu', 'different', and she writes as an Outsider of the land and the people, mostly the people. Not having a common language, she watches people closely and with compassion of their lives and their deaths. Irma is a great storyteller and her poetry has a wonderful clarity. Irma has left her own river and finds, in this new river of Africa, 'fullness and beauty'."

— Peter L. Evans, Poets Anonymous.

Red Winds – The Full Reviews

"This is a personal record of heart-wrenching experiences told by an honest woman, Ms. Irma Upex-Huggins. She is respectful to the people she was privileged to work with. She felt their pain, shared their grief, and identified with their sufferings.

Ms. Upex-Huggins a mental health social worker, was a Voluntary Service Overseas (VSO) worker among the Wanyamwezi people of Tanzania, in the mid 1990's. VSO, an international development agency, is committed to a 'world without poverty'. It is therefore not surprising that those professionals like Irma, who worked with the organization, would have a similar commitment.

However, here is a unique perspective, from a brave, determined and courageous woman, who sees the 'red winds' with different eyes. Eyes informed by a deep-seated African retention that connects her with Africa's peoples and cultures. In these 102 pages we find a combination of biography, travel log and poetic exuberance.

Ms. Upex-Huggins portrays the human face behind the de-personalised statistics, political machinations and international policies often raised when discussing Tanzania's high infant mortality, sparse health services, low literacy rate and limited rural development. Off the tourist routes, she introduces us to a living that is simple yet culturally complex. Danger, excitement, fear, joy, anger, hope and homesickness are all encased in this anthology.

Although Tanzania experienced relatively rapid growth in per capita Gross Domestic Product in the last half of the 1990's and showed a modest decline in poverty, Ms. Upex-Huggins insight reveals the true nature of the quality of life for most rural women in Tanzania in that same period. The worldview and tenacity of the people she encountered can be imagined in 'Prayers from the Shamba', a time of famine, and then torrential rains and destructive floods in 'I hear my cattle bawling.' Such is the nature of life in many developing countries that the vulnerable rural poor and emaciated children refuse to bow to despair.

Tanzania was one of the top recipients of overseas development aid during the period 1996-1998. It is reassuring to know that there are ordinary women and men from all across the world willing to serve others irrespective of the risks to themselves. Here is one such soul who served needy humanity with her eyes of compassion and love. This 'inquisitive observer of people looking in from outside' helps us, who are outside, to look in."

— Ronald A. Nathan is a local church minister, public theologian and Pan- Africanist, who has travelled extensively on the African continent, the Americas and Europe.

RED WINDS
A VSO in Tanzania

Red Winds – A VSO in Tanzania

Published by Palewell Press Ltd
http://www.palewellpress.co.uk/

First Edition

ISBN 978-1-911587-07-1

A CIP catalogue record for this title is available from the British Library.

Palewell Press

RED WINDS
A VSO in Tanzania

Poems and prose by

Irma Upex-Huggins

Dedication

Dedicated to Michael C Worsley
Science Teacher
VSO (1966-1967)
Charlestown Secondary School
Nevis, West Indies

Michael Worsley brought a richness to our school and island community. He inspired and encouraged young minds to look to our futures with passion.

Thanks

To George Wright who supported and encouraged me throughout my VSO experience: before and after Tanzania. Although VSO was part of a life plan, it was none-the-less a painful experience leaving family and home for two years. George's letters, telephone calls, visits, were of great comfort and encouragement, particularly when I was struggling with malaria or on return home for treatment, following the bus accident. He held 'home' for me: caring for Koko and Bundi, our dogs and giving supportive guidance to my sons. He is actively helpful to me in putting this collection together.

This book is for Edgar, Billy and Richard, my sons, with love.

Special thanks also to:
- Reverend Adelyn Mgonela (Pastor Moravian Church, Eastern West Indies Province), formerly a Missionary Nursing Sister at Moravian Church Western Tanzania (MCWT), Tabora.
- The Milumbani Women's Group (MCWT) who included me in the sisterhood of Tanzanian women.

- Mzee Nsimba who was key to my work in understanding and communicating with different cultural groups in village communities. He was sensitive about me not eating meat (chicken is cooked to welcome visitors) and sent 'the message' ahead of visits. He was with me in the bus crash and helped me come through the trauma.
- Dr. Ringo, Consultant Psychiatrist, Mirembe Hospital & Isanga Institution, Dodoma, who provided a three-week work experience giving me invaluable insights into Tanzania Mental Health Services.
- Dorothy, Peter and Michael who all kept me safe and well at my home in Tabora.

With thanks to my publisher, Camilla Reeve, who held the pages of Red Winds with care and wrapped them together with skill.

Using colours as metaphor, Tanzania 1996–1998

In 1996, I was working as a VSO* in Tanzania. I travelled to remote villages and worked in communities sometimes for up to two weeks, so witnessed people's hospitality and generosity first hand. As a stranger, I was received with a heartfelt "Karibu" * and a willingness to share what little that people had. I worked closely with individual women and groups, gained valuable insights into gender roles and observed women being powerful without usurping men's place and authority.

My poems aim to reflect the rhythms and spirit of 'traditional' Tanzania through its harsh beauty, situations and vibrant colours. In 1996, Tanzania was reported as the 'second poorest country' in the world, despite its abundant natural resources. People lived harmonious, resourceful and hopeful lives. There were over 120 traditional groups, many of whom converted to Muslim and Christian faiths. (I lived with the Nyamwezi people. I was also given the name "Njoki", which means, "She who returned"). Kiswahili is the national language with English used for external communications. Codes of conduct were linked to the Muslim faith, in terms of modesty in dress, gender roles; relationships, rites etc. Small numbers of tribal groups retained their languages and cultural traditions.

Water impacted hugely on lives, particularly in rural communities, where scarcity and contamination were linked to malaria, other water-borne diseases, crop failures and mortality rates. In times of floods, crops are ruined, communities cut off, washed away, people and animals face starvation and death. In 1997, parts of Tanzania suffered severe flooding and newspapers reported hungry lions entering villages, dragging people away. I witnessed the 1997 floods, the destruction to lives, the scarring of landscapes, saw desert areas turned into rivers, and men catching fish on what had been land. Other parts of the country however, experienced drought and threats to livelihoods.

Tanzania is naturally beautiful, harsh and untamed. Mt Kilamanjaro, Ngorongoro Crater, Saa Nane, The Great Lakes, Zanzibar (Unguja and Pemba,), the wild animals, birds, spices, bush medicines, give the country its unique beauty and colour.

After finishing my placement, I travelled 'rough' looking for adventure before returning home. I travelled alone by lorries, trains, bus, motorbike, boat. Once I held a dead baby as the mother climbed in the lorry. I witnessed how people live, and the effects of sameness and difference of tradition. I watched a man from my train window, carrying a dead body on his shoulder to put on the train. I spoke sufficient Kiswahili to travel without difficulty. My experiences were varied and interesting. I was not deterred by ever present dangers (poorly maintained transport, loose speeding laws, bad roads) in travelling around the country. Women are respected in Tanzania. I always took appropriate care for my own safety. Nevertheless, in August 1996, I was involved in a serious crash when travelling home from working in Igunga, a village 145 kilometres from Tabora. VSO made sure I was well enough to continue my work 'in-country and offered 6 weeks treatment back in England. In my first week back in Tanzania, I was travelling in Dar es Salaam by Dala-Dala (minibus). Travelling by Dala-Dala is always a 'tight squeeze' and only when the bus is full will it leave the terminus, picking up people all the way to its destination. I was held in place by the squash of bodies, as it sped through the streets. A thought that if there was a crash, I would be thrown out and killed, was soon brushed from my mind. In Tanzania, whether travel was by road, train, or by sea, 'overcrowding' was always an issue. In addition to this trauma, I was sick with malaria five times and, on one occasion, this was along with paratyphoid. When the placement ended, I was seven and a half stones of skin and bones. I left my own river, the many times I cried, the many times I laughed and laughed.

As a black woman I felt Tanzania, 'through my navel-string'. Some cultural practices held powerful meanings for me. Caribbean childhood memories were triggered just watching people go about their lives (The Tea Seller; Night Train from Kigoma To Dar es Salaam). My poetry aims to bring alive raw Tanzania in colour, sound and smell.

The poems are written with a Caribbean swing and slang; e.g. "wen yuh ban yuh belly an bawl" * is an expression of extreme grief, for example, at the loss of a child and, deliberately, do not follow conventional uses of grammar.

Irma Upex-Huggins

*VSO * - Voluntary Service Overseas*

Contents

Mama Tanzania - One

I struggle inside the tangles
this cloth you lay before me
this symbol signal me to turn
the colours inside out
I struggle inside the tangles
the intimacy, the misery
the daily rites for your dead
I do not want dried up breasts
your hanging helplessness

Mama, big with child again
and malaria still chose
who live who die
accusation or judgement
the seal can be broken
for less than a penny a day

where is water for your crops
water safe for your child
day by day your grave-song
leave an impotent sting
in my throat

your crops burn up in the sun
drown in the revenge of rain
I fear the empty table.

Mama Tanzania - Two
(For Dorothy: a late, late response after talking with a Missionary)

fashioned by a passionate sun
so quick upon birth you
leave your father's house
we sisters prepare you
for the journey
perfume thick, black lips
boil tea, put in cardamom
prepare you for the name
every breath will honour
at the meaning bow
name that mother a continent
mama is praise-song
in wind, over ocean
in your mountains, on your plains
wen yuh ban yuh belly an bawl
parched lands turn rivers, crops fail.

mama, I did not stop the missionary
when his lies nailed you to the cross, I stepped aside
as he slashed your body, pierced your soul, I left as
he embalmed you in the religion of a hateful tongue
prophets come, vomit falsehoods, lay curses on you
for the hunger, for the dying, the ravages of your land
your bleeding will call to account those who persecute
make dumb their mouths, red with souls they crucify.

Ghosts at a traditional dance

ngoma seep deep in my soul
reach memory
touch Africa inside
ngoma strip me, shake me
I the exile dance
dance the sacrifice
dance this market-place
dance this people-trade
the gold for plastic beads
I a stolen people
I a price paid
I flesh, I blood
I ghosts of sons
I ghosts of daughters
I dance the story

I desire you red winds
you undulating hills
move me
dance me
skin of my skin
flesh of my flesh
black without waste on bones

Tanzania
dance my coming home
dance my soul o my soul
dance me in the meaning.

Night Train from Kigoma to Dar es Salaam

twisting and winding through lives
where a cool inter-city is far country
here people-herds run to meet
the night train from Kigoma
Lake Tanganyika fade
a memory now the night
travellers turn to conversation

five and twenty carriages haul moments along
a blue farewell and cicadas sing in the cantata
panting people with kerosene lamps run to food
- stops, wait line-side, yellow light touching night
show lives as trawling nets on this shore
bananas that displease are tossed back
like dead fish

travellers pick off your diamonds
missionaries warn of the evil poor
say the night is full of thieves

I listen to curses
hear the night mocking
lamplight show shilingi
a shining in the sand
I see faces
ghosts of another time
scrabbling for pennies
tourists toss in the dirt.

Prayers from the shamba

Is three years
Lord send rain
for the shamba
for the thirsty ground
the dust dry, my hand weary
the sun is burning up the corn
and still they stand respectful
in their famine queues
in dreams dried-up
no going to mill
no wedding flour
still my faithful soul
pray prayers
perform rites
I am scratching hope
staving off the hunger
as I wait for a miracle
to come from the sky.

Flamingos in a pink horizon

like the diamonds of our country
a hidden fire rage
when money gods come hunting here
our fertile pastures turn to pleasure lands
and we are hostage to drought, to flood
our eyes full of malaria are too weak
to dam your lies, your after-dinner jokes
the man who wash your smelly drawers
to pay bride-price, you call him houseboy

progress want dirt off my face
my culture to wear new clothes
to show no wounding scars

I am energy of grateful hands
the scorch on your safari tales
I am Ngorongoro, Kilimanjaro
mountain stones of Saa Nane
I block the sun on killer weeds
sucking life from Lake Victoria
I hear songs
frogs singing after rain
I fly wild
a beautiful rage
untamed in red
pink&ocean-blue
jacaranda purple
black, rose-gold
in a pink horizon.

Malaria

I am burning up
in strange fever
degedege
rattle the bones
I hear my mlinzi
mumbling Swahili
his praying is late
God abandoned me
to voices in my head
outside night is
an oilskin cover
creeping round
round and round
inside my head
is unfamiliar rain

a war
quinine and malaria
quinine is scooping
tossing out
scooping
tossing out
inside my head
a rattling galvanise
is shaking loose
I fear this trembling
tossing now to ghosts
sequestrating dead cells.

After the Tanzanian sunset

Homesick - One

I am hunted in this night
give me light for the road
so I do not loose my foot
I cannot see the dream
give back morning rising
black edges on rose-gold
slow seconds
black edges
yolk-yellow centre
softening to light
till light finger Dar es Salaam

after you roll
in a gold ball
night move fast
wrap up leftovers
pale colours
the last passion
vex the smile
drop the after-glow in the sea.

Homesick - Two

I say to you red winds
now a total blackness
resurrect the dreaming
from the drowning sea
promise sleep so I dream of Kariakoo
colours, smells, the squash of people
in the marketplace
blow me shouting streets of Dar es Salaam
speeding dala-dalas through this loneliness
the moon is absent
the dark accusing
stretching out like a buzzing mosquito
condemning me to night without stars
I see no ghosts, I see no dreams
I hear no guitars, your beginning.

Night Fishing on Lake Nyasa in rain season

a wild crying blind night, blot out the stars
blackness cover all between lake and sky
light from the lamp is weak, the oil too little
to help fishermen lure degaa

the unforgiving rain
hauling all to the lake
drag down mountains
drown roads

no mercy for fishermen
who cannot walk on water
but must find oil for light
to see the night through

night will avenge dry lanterns
when the light go out, is dead
dawn rising will mock empty nets
expose the reluctant canoes
that must row home without food
past the judgement of crocodiles.

Glimpses of the Ngorongoro

The Lions

if you forget where you are
like in a dream or sleeping
as you walk in wild savanna dreams
you will meet lions of The Ngorongoro
in long grass lying down or hunting, or
if you are lying down in your front room
you will meet lions of The Ngorongoro
as you watch a David Attenborough

the sun is hot
jeeps on safari give shade
lions cool out
just lying there
in the front room
your granny will be taking
homemade lemonade to cool down

and you will forgive her
if she bends to stroke
she might be thinking
it is one of those big brown dogs
she is not sure what breed of Alsatian.

Watch out for Eagles

this is your lunch stop
in this place eagles watch from trees
will take aim, swoop down as you eat
grab your lunch and fly off

eating in The Ngorongoro
is safe
safer in a pack of people
eagles watch from trees

when an eagle marks you
and swoops down, let go
or by your lunch you will
go flying through the sky
holding one end of a paper bag
the eagle holding the other end

when you no longer hear the wind
feel a flapping up and down
when the eagle wipes his beak
kicks shredded paper from feet
you will drop

eating in The Ngorongoro
is safe
safer in a pack of people
eagles watch from trees.

Ngriti

a curious looking flash in the sun
or a rotund beauty on short legs
dainty, moving fast and
to eyes unaccustomed
the warthog is close, almost ugly
short sight, oversensitive hearing
tusks, two pairs on a long mouth
a short pair dig for food, long ones
fearsome weapons challenge lions
antenna tail end a red-brown
curling from the neckline
running, never trusting
and will suddenly stop
to shake his head
grunt displeasure
suspicion in his eyes
predators everywhere
are bothering his nose
suddenly he runs off
antenna tail whirling
ears up
then suddenly a stop
suspicion in his eyes.

Late Thoughts: after a night in Ugali Reserve
(Tabora Region)

a foolishness to sleep with lions
in an abandoned concrete space
one park ranger to guard us
one oil lamp in the darkness
keep out snakes crawling in

a room with roof and four walls
a window cut-out, a cut-out door
or money run out on half-cooked
plan or scheming
five lives will sleep
in that foolishness

or the romance of
a ranger with rifle
important and starched
in khaki uniform

I know the park ranger
has no bullets in the rifle
at his side. In the collusion
he will be free to eat for two days

the driver and mate gather firewood
fish in the river, dodge crocodiles on patrol
start a fire to last through the night, roast the
fish on hot yellow tongues that lick them till sweet

in feverish excitement
I lie listening to lions
praying for a distance far
mosquitoes buzz nearer
outside the net hung for
protection from malaria

lions did not come
we champions rise
triumphant in the morning
I knead flour, fry dumplin
the driver and mate cook ugali
we eat, drink chai, go off on safari
tsetse flies following bite out blood
as we push the stalling bus through sand.

Night Safari in a Game Reserve
a night of entente cordial

as if singing sign up people
and wild beasts in the night
orange flickering show faces
on safari in an animal world

hyenas sing contributions in high pitched
melodies, throaty callings from bull-frogs
on cool river banks mix in the shallow breathing
of crocodiles in the silent dancing light of fireflies

and as if night is calling time
on the slaughter of elephants
on the yellow spite of malaria
in the eye of tomorrow.

I hear my cattle bawling

the rain did not want to come
stayed away years and years
today vengeance came down
plundered me and my house
took all, the rain showing no mercy
I hear my cattle in a drowning distance
bawling like wind tearing into flapping sail

this year the rain root out the corn
drown all, wash away everything
before today years were burning
drying up all the corn, and
all the dried up corn fall down dead
poor land never know who is coming
poor land know only the guest is king

in rain, rain, rain, I hear my cattle bawling
yesterday hot winds blew scorching sands
scurrying scorpions were crossing deserts
yesterday's deserts are cooling rivers now
rivers full of fish
rain pierce the mountains
red water run from their sides
starving lions go into villages
take out lives
all I own is gone in the rain
I hear my cattle in a drowning distance
bawling like wind tearing into flapping sail.

The Boy from the Refugee Camp in Kigoma

did not belong to anyone
looked no more than ten
had no school no church
no mosque, followed me

in Kigoma marketplace
weaving shampoo in a dance
in, out the market maduka
he on the opposite side

Africa sun glue our days
me, he
tourist and refugee
reflections on the shadow

from a distance I watch umbrellas
the everyday crossings on The Lake
colours of a people escaping genocide
hiding from the sun

I watch lives
overcrowding
Nduta Refugee Camp

I watch his hope
to escape
soldiers in town
rounding up with guns

I peel off
the burden
on my freedom.

Black Mzungu

just the way I walk
hair flowing
black, copper colour
at sunburned edges

tight blue jeans
declaring seven stones
astride a Suzuki
pikipiki

no Tanzania woman walk
like if she owns the streets
men stand aside
as I pass

swahili-english
stagger cross
from Tabora Market
"mama, kuja",
"Morogoro pineapple"

I wave, shout a greeting
"jambo, tuonane kesho"
come out lumpy
like how I cook ugali

a malicious somebody
throw stones
after all
I am a woman.

Dollar in my pocket

the shopkeeper includes me
in the mzungu circle
the dollar in my pocket
is access to gossip
my pass to hear news
not privilege to black ears

last night
a house-girl
poison her mistress food

I hear the news ring
out, revolution come
to root out humiliation
I hear the bells
I hear the news
the news bring cry-water
to my eye, wash my face
I stir more poison in
more cries, more poison
loud alarms, more poison
cries mouthing outrage
raising false sympathies
outpourings of a glad heart.

Searching out someone else's rubbish
as if it's your time now

this time, someone else's rubbish
is potato peelings in my backyard
half cooked bread I throw away
you dig out in the dead of night

in darkness you dig out my excesses
my more than enough, my throwaways
you separating kitchen from bathroom
remind me

of Thursday nights, me rummaging through
other people's rubbish put out for collection
finding worn carpet to cover a cold linoleum
bringing home an old coat to keep winter out

I searched side-streets, over walls
returned empty beer bottles to pubs
the pennies landlords paid was little
but helped put food on the table.

Bicycles in Tabora

after church, I sit side saddle going home
a yellow blowing turn a black face blacker
a dreaming open colours of a peacock fan
in a rickshaw evening down the kings road

my rider navigates holes in the red dirt road
criss-crossing the roughly hacked out codes
unspoken secrets in eyes, in a waiting ready
to drag infraction down onto begging knees

bicycles that were icons in last century China
are beasts of burden in 21st century Tabora
bicycles fit seasons, customs, every tradition
and will not die from hunger, drought or flood

a bicycle will be faithful to the man who carries
two wives and their hoes to shamba every day
and his bicycle will not be weary
and his bicycle will not grow thin.

Body wrapped up, unseen

he knows it will pass
rolled up as carpet on his shoulder
he walking with a body wrapped up
will go unnoticed to the train

all the dead must return to their ancestral home
it is custom. With the money all spent on treatment
the man will walk through Dar es Salaam hot streets
enter 3rd class on the train that will carry Mzee home

on the bustling railway station only the foreigner see
a raised eyelid acknowledging the complex churning
of life in slow motion, no questions asked, this body
now is baggage cotching-up in a corner on the train

and as if the silence answer, "hakuna matata"
somewhere between Dar es Salaam and Kigoma
in thick night or in a fiery tomorrow
a man with a body will step down from the train.

The Waterman

when I drink chai
rangi or maziwa
in the morning, or
take tea in the afternoon
with cardamom perfume
I think of the waterman

going up, down
up, down in boiling sun
walking hours
pushing cart
in this village, that town
bringing water to people
going on safari

earning little
few shilingi
selling water
in hotels, in homes
to people untangling
mosquito nets, buying
water they bathe in

he walked the years, barefoot
now he wears redundant tyres
recycled for shoes
tyres that battled desert sands
tyres that lived patch-up lives
on dangerous roads
bus tyres, car tyres.

Stillborn

I watch her crying
behind empty eyes
not looking on
her stillborn
not watching
not seeing her self
truncated, distanced
she is obedient
believe in myths
Christian-Muslim
herbs, bones
magic nights
in no moon

"pole" tumble out
foreign, feeble, not knowing
if fate or if offence
or if tradition ordain that she
should look into the distance
no tears, no touching
her child that come too early

the man must dig a grave
for this symbolic planting
for the child to come back
in another pregnancy
"God-willing"
in a second coming
"God-willing"
the child will come back live
the child that come too early.

Looking for Lake Nyasa Crocodiles

when somebody say
mzungu just come
off the back of a lorry

he waited outside
the lutheran courtyard
in the changing times

new missionaries now
come to metema beach
to hunt crocodiles
not preach

he paddled his canoe
she photographed a man
shouting shilingi, shilingi
mbaya uso, she teased

there were no crocodiles
no tossing heads
no snapping jaws
no upside down fore-play
maybe they were allowing
the foolish mzungu to pass
watching from reed beds.

The Tea Seller

walk up and down, a
coal-pot on her head
orange fire boiling tea
she walk up and down
up, down
the station
calling out
"chai", "chai"
intermittently
walking up, down
up, down making life
making life selling tea
cardamom drag my nose
in-between people and train

memory turn back time
position my head
balance a bucket
give permission to laugh.

Without Words

even when the sky is black
I travel alone in language
I watch people, imitate myths
practise superstitions, interpret

signs, a silence begging me to hold
her baby wrapped in grave clothes
I held her empty eyes, held the pain
held the tradition behind a dry crying

I sit, swing a foot in train door-ways
at food-stops on the line. Inquisitive, I
learn the language of travel and trade
a clinking shilingi or a crude bartering

faces at the window teeth-brushing is
morning language on the overnight train
I copy the imagination, spit out mischief
with the spittle I watch flying in the wind

a hole in the floor
call a careful foot
astride the ordure
a language I learn without words.

Cooking up a celebration

after we carry water
to fill up
cut-down
oil-drums

fetch firewood
choose three stones
for every cooking pot
light the fire

grind peanuts for sauce
wash spinach
cook chicken
each woman taking turns
paddling rice with wooden spoons

for vegetarian
without translation
we cook red beans

we eat by firelight
call ghosts by wood-smoke
we dance in the swirling grey
our laughter seducing the night.

All travellers have dirty fingernails

woman alone going on safari

30 hours by bus
Tabora to Arusha
is a journey crossing hell
red winds blow, dust fly unbroken
settle in wigs, eyebrows, wrapped hair
under fingernails, in faces
one side first
I look again into a deeper ochre mix
of dust on the many shades of black skin
see markings of tales to tell later
yesterday death tumble over in slow motion
the treacherous landscape show no sign
we hack our way through ugly scaring
the red covering of time

we lean side to side
eyes silent
children roadside sing
"gari", "gari"
and
hand-dance
s-shape girls wedge babies
in hip-bone curves
they have no dolls
steal time to play

three hundred miles
crush karibu
crumble safari njema
amnesiac clouds offend
toilet decorum
"sorry, sorry"
erase
samahami.

woman going home

kwaheri Arusha, I go into the night
into ominous stares
into tragedy on the bus-roof pile high
into cables hissing

inside the gas station
the driver lights his cigarette
fill up the bus
puffs smoke
inside the bus I die
ambushed by death
while 'fatalities prevention' sleep
I see my end.

I sleep, wake
in a speeding nightmare
in a forest high
in a total night
in the bus light
trees are
tombstones-people
standing in a circle
I see my funeral.

in voices loud and long
goats and cocks call morning
the sun marinade man and beasts
roast the bodies
a woman holds a red cock on her lap
catch droppings in a plastic bag
the bus groans
stops
people squat in naked sand
grab 15 stinking toilet minutes in towns.

no, I will not marry you

I want to reach home
before the bus falls
sun drinks my blood
sand hide the bones
and love's memorial
where will that be
with no ashes
no bones.

Time flowing slowly

I enjoy hours sitting alone
in the heart of River Temi
the water now in no hurry
as if picking up my mood
Mt Meru meet my eyes
wrap her beauty round me
sounds tumbling over rocks
play for my ears
here and there water seep out
slowly, at first more like a stain
on the ground
before joining bigger waters
running past me wondering
about the stones
I sit watching people in the distance
passing on the other side, going home.

Writing home

son, so much of life here is tied
to traditional way of doing things
to policy and procedure I forget
but "the guest is king"

still I am 'an outsider'
put in the 'mzungu corner'
with issues: faults, things foreign
punishment for not talking swahili

I forget the 2 months booking
for 1st class to Dar es Salaam
when the train from Kigoma
groan to a stop in Tabora

I jump in 3rd class
no ticket, no space
knees in face, near a
man choking on malaria

in shaking fear, maybe fever
pompous and in lieu of ticket
present myself as "guest" at
the invitation of the president

/continued

the guard welcome me
to 1st class
that lie grab my mouth, shackle my tongue
I could not speak till we reach Dar es Salaam.

*   *   *

Dar es Salaam to Tabora by plane
sixteen thousand feet and climbing
a white Alsatian watch in silence
from a cage in the tail of the plane

in the chaos
a steward struggle
to shut the stuffed
overhead bin-door

the dog is French I hear
understands no swahili
we watch, eyes silent
tongues still

I wonder if we will
make it to Tabora
with three people
squeezed in two seats

did not make it last time
after dancing off and on
early one morning
till late afternoon

I poor dancer
out of rhythm
keeping step

protest
without trumpet
or words
to the press

at end of the day we were asleep in cosy opulence
but familiar sounds of Dar es Salaam were missing
in the morning. There was no waiting, no ringing
no running to the sounds of Jeshi la Wokovu bells.

Eating together

there are rituals before eating
and, to the two Tanzanian men

now house-guests in my country
I will say "karibu" as I pour water
so they wash their hands
in a traditional welcome

traditional roles
where do they fit in this part of London
the answer of course is not compulsory
even in my house

my sister-friends
will not kneel before men
pour water for their hands

inside the politics of woman
is the algebra of traditional
roles and symbols and
this night will be judge
will answer that which has meaning
only in itself, has no meaning outside

I prepare a table for my guests
the night hold judgement as we women
honour the custom of traditional sisters
hold the symbolisms of hand washing
pour a traditional welcome to the table
the judgement of the night.

The woman in black

all day for years she leans
she is a black outline
a wall-statue on the bank
in the centre of Tabora
a queen in islamic dress
every pore of her skin
every fibre of the cloth
is a painting in used oil
her arms on head curl
she is part of the wall
when she is not there
she leaves her outline
the shape of her absence
head-foot-breasts-belly-space
as if a monument missing
taken out for cleaning
I never meet her eyes
never see her come
never see her go

when she is not there
she leaves her pattern
as if for conversation
with feelings come up inside yourself
about the empty space, the something
missing, a memorial stone taken away
gone, and to where, you have no news
who she is no one knows
or where she goes to when she leaves
she comes, goes as silent as a soft wind.

Hard choices

she gave birth to a baby girl
when the hospital could not
stop her bleeding
she died
she did not have
sufficient money
she could not afford
the whole cost
the drugs for a safe birth
had to 'chance it'
she gambled, lost, died
and the baby
just out of the womb
wait in a kanga
giving hope and fate
equal chance to decide
equal time to make a plan.

he could only afford to collect
the body of his own daughter
for a traditional burying
to satisfy the ancestors
cannot afford another mouth
a baby cannot work to earn
he must leave her
his granddaughter, her daughter
he must leave her in the hospital.

nurse may take her
raise her as her own
or it is her fate to die
he cannot afford more food.

After the bus crash
(a poem for George)

I look for her on the road
I cannot find my love
My love has left the road

I look for my love amongst
the blood, the broken bones
My love is not with the dead

I look for her in the will of God
I search the wreckage
the Sodom and Gomorrah
She is not there

I do not know where my love has gone

I look for her in the psychiatrist's chair
My love is not there

I look for her running naked in the wind
I hold back raging rivers
dig through desert sands

I look for her in the
fate of being poor
She is not there

I look for her with the pink flamingos
on the crystal lake

I look for her in the clouds
that sit on Kilimanjaro
I do not find her

on the plains of Ngorongoro
in the waters of Lake Manyara
I do not find her

I walk along the Rift Valley
walk the Milky Way
I do not find her

I look for her on the road
the journey she began
I do not find her

I look into my heart
She is there.

The Witch

pushing his water-cart up the path
find me sitting in evening half-light
locks of African hair
snatch his mind
fix his eyes, tell him I am
"one of those evil ones
who live in the woods
who come out at night
to suck human blood"
hiding now in half-light
he back-back
back-back slow
lock eyes till out of sight
he's running in my mind
running fast, faster-faster
I feel fear bubbling inside
a memory
a stolen people story
a past weighing heavy
come, I am not mchawi
I am a woman
like you, I am African
it is time we come together
to understand the meaning
this choir prepare for Easter
we can sit down and together
break bread and drink wine.

Learning to ride motorcycle
on the psychological road to Tanzania

They ran two by two the men
to pick up bits of motorcycle
the shape of clutch control
for a perfect figure of eight
lovers concern
were broken bits of bone
that add together dreams
knitting equations
take away sums
not logic or easy to understand
when love is a jigsaw, a hope
in aching hearts, almost breaking
fragile on the finishing line.

How many hearts desire Tanzania
to take you away from Croydon
knots if many lovers
the consequences if more than one
reveal complications of love affairs
bruises from the fall will cover for pain
given that more than two men
will be the answer to that test
there is no CBT for purple thumbs
swelling out at irregular triangles or
outside the competence of grey hairs
there is a time for perfecting triangles
time past to ride continents in the sand.

Take off your red shoes

I leave all behind
in my red shoes
on the doorstep
I am going home

I leave behind innocence
a million dead bodies
a black-ants invasion
I did not understand

I leave behind sand brushed from a boy leading an old man
leave the 12-foot stick, grind to dust the comedy of over-size
custard-bright-yellow-frame-black-lens-charity-sunglasses
school that will abandon mzee to begging help in his world.

I leave behind a blind woman travelling to her future
a suckling child on the breast she leaves hanging out
she has dreams for start-up projects, business plans
I leave behind women planting roots of sustainability.

I leave behind the full gospel, faith in deliverance from evil
the twenty-four hands on the head of the boy on his knees
twelve believers in a circle who are shaking out shetani
chanting "not epileptic", driving out pure evil from this boy.

I leave behind night thumping, screaming, bawling
holding on to secrets: consultations with wachawi
for myths of good fortune, the magic of dead bones
the cleansing potions, drinking cures under darkness

I leave behind faith marking the door with
a cross to save the first born from malaria
life and death is everyday
a celebration, a mourning

I leave behind symbols
the henna painted hands
the preacher say "wash it
off, this is not Christian."

she wipes vomit in her kanga
it touches me I do not care
I am walking away from the
wreck of lives on the road

I leave behind a John the Baptist, naked in the marketplace
he is shaking a dried-up snake as a warning or
driving out evil spirits or divining, nobody cares
at closing time, he will return to his home in the caves

I leave behind hard questions of greater need
x-ray generator or psychiatric drugs or stronger
restraints or bigger budgets for rice and beans
I leave behind Tanzania in my red shoes.

Letters from Tabora

May 1996

The Road to Tabora was long with always the taste of wild honey. As I take you down this Road, I hope I capture the romance of Tanzania.

In 1966, I was privileged to be taught Science by a VSO Volunteer who came to Nevis to work at Charlestown Secondary School for one year. This experience greatly influenced my life leaving an indelible imprint of service, given with love, humility and altruism.

In 1968, I left the Caribbean and later realised why I wanted to work as a VSO. Growing up in the Caribbean, I was aware of whisperings about families with a 'fooly pickney', a child who had mental or physical difficulties. Myths and fantasies would develop around 'causes', and people were reluctant to marry into 'bad blood'. These children were often 'hidden away' in their family homes.

My dream burned with new fire and in 1981, I was sure that I no longer wanted to work in the Caribbean. I felt drawn to be a 'volunteer' in Africa with deep and unexplained feelings to work in Ghana. My grandfather was called Sakie and I learned that the name is common in a specific region in Ghana. When my father confirmed that our roots were in Ghana, I decided to be a 'volunteer' in that country, but, God had other plans.

Through the years, family and friends helped to keep the 'dream' alive. I got encouragement and support from my sister Jackie, my cousin Coralie, my sister-friend Joy and Michael Jackson (VSO Ethiopia 1965), former minister of my home church, Brighton Road Baptist. Talks with

Michael helped me explore volunteering from a Christian perspective. My sons, Edgar, Billy and Richard, shared 'the dream', giving me the freedom of being mother, without the pain of torn loyalties. George's love, on which I continue to depend, is patient. His support for my work is silent, strong and rich in selfless giving. He too is making a long journey.

When I was welcomed into the church family (Moravian Church in Western Tanzania) MCWT*, I dedicated my commitment to work in the community with a reading from 2 Peter: 4: 10-11, reminding myself of the responsibilities of being "a good manager of God's gifts", to "…use these gifts for the good of others…" and to "…serve with the strength God gives…"

I brought good memories with me from England: the goodbye celebrations which Andrea, Ekenam, Lonsdale and Marcia organised with poetry and rhythms of Africa: Audrey and a Brother, honouring me with the Drum; words of encouragement from Anna-Marie, Dr Adjin-Tetey, Gillian, Philip, the farewell from my sons and George, the gentle touching from friends, the hugs without words, Andrea tending my hair. The supper George prepared for us was reminiscent of an even greater event.

The journey from England was uneventful until we arrived in Kenya. After passengers had disembarked, we were told that our British Airways 747, had developed engine problems. We were periodically given "the good news" and "the bad news": the plane was working but the electricity at the airport was down. Six hours later we were on our way to Dar es Salaam. The journey had taken eighteen hours: the whole time being spent in the aircraft.

The drive through Dar es Salaam from the airport was a culture shock. I had read reports that Tanzania was the second poorest country in the world and I was now seeing what that meant. One of my first experiences was a feeling of belonging, 'of coming home'. Despite this, however, here in Tabora, I often get the feeling of living in a zoo when walking up the streets, with the wind blowing through my beautiful hair, with everything about my walk and dress saying I am a stranger.

My decision not to give money to beggars was challenged early on my arrival in Tanzania. On my way to Tabora, I was sitting on Dodoma Station waiting for the train when a small boy leading a blind and infirm old man stopped and stood in front of me, repeating, "saidia" (help). I ignored them, unsure that this was a charitable response. I experienced the encounter as an uncomfortable burden.

Part of our 'Language and Culture' Induction was a five-days 'Family Stay'. Given choice, I would not have chosen experiencing 'family life' after only two weeks in the country. I was not emotionally ready to live in a family home whilst feeling vulnerable, and, without a common language. However, this turned out to be an invaluable learning and humbling time. In sharing the family's life, I gained a new and different meaning of "God is everywhere". Even though 'my family' said grace before each meal, at that time I would have found it unthinkable that God would choose to be in a cockroach-infested community: filled with malnourished children with yellow-white silent eyes. It was a great comfort to realise that God did not stay just with the clean and well fed! I was shown hospitality by my family and other families I met, enriched by experiencing the poverty from which it came.

During 'The Stay', I became ill and started vomiting one morning, as I walked to classes. When I began crying, a small group of concerned women surrounded me, worried that it was 'my heart', and saying "pole" (condolences), to comfort me. Fortunately, I was walking with four other women volunteers, who were staying with families in the area. They helped me, and I was taken to the doctor, suffering with memory confusion and raging headaches. My memory was clear two days later, and I recalled having sat in the sun without head covering. I suffered another shock - discovering that I lost TSh 40,000 (Tanzanian Shillings). On my way to the 'family-stay, I removed the money from my kanga wrap to buy a gift for 'my family' but failed, afterwards to secure it properly in the folds of the material. This was almost half my monthly allowance of TSh 90,000. I was left with 150 shillingi, which is less than the price of a soda. Fortunately, on the same day, VSO provided us with three months' allowances, as we were soon leaving Dar for our placements 'up-country'. In coming to terms with the loss, I felt able to bear it as no other loss could compare with that of separation from my family in the UK. I prayed that the money would be useful to whoever found it.

Before leaving Dar, I want to tell you that there were many good and positive experiences, and I did have fun. Kivukoni Fish Market in Dar, the largest one in Tanzania, was an exciting place to visit with its smells and beautiful array of colours and sizes: of lobsters, crabs, prawns, fish, turtle shells, sharks-teeth and other strange creatures from the sea, I had never seen before. One could buy for a banquet and still have change from £5. I also enjoyed the pleasure of looking out onto the Indian Ocean from the cool of palm trees, over what seemed like miles and miles of white sand. One morning I watched dhows come ashore and witnessed more than fifty women wearing brightly coloured kangas (two pieces of cloth, one used as a wrap-round skirt, the other for a shawl or head-dress) with baskets on their heads walking across the sand to the dhows. The women were collecting fish for the Market. Biblical images came to my mind and I imagined that this was what it looked like with the five thousand, going to hear Jesus preach!

THE DALA-DALA EXPERIENCE is a must when in Dar. One would miss the taste of the City without a ride on one of these 'death traps'. A 'Dala-Dala' is a small private bus which is usually painted in bright and bold colours. Each bus has its own unique and witty name, written in its own big and bold style. Dala-Dalas are used to make short journeys in and around towns and cities and in Dar, they travel at frightening speeds and make screeching sounds when they stop. These buses never leave from one destination to the other without being 'sardine-packed'. A bus is never full: if there are people, there is space. Buses are operated by a driver and conductor – the 'collector' of the 'shilingi mia moja' (one hundred shillingi) fare. Conductors 'swing' (a way of standing on the steps) on the outside of the Dala-Dala, calling out loudly their destination, such as "POSTA" "POSTA" or "KARIAKOO", "KARIAKOO". There is no such thing as 'personal space' and when travelling on a

Dala-Dala, there is only 'breathing room and body contact' space. For one not used to travelling in this way it is, initially, a very uncomfortable feeling. No one abuses this intimate contact, however.

There is not much public touching between men and women, just the briefest of a handshake (the right hand always offered), is an acceptable form of greeting. It is also acceptable for men to hold hands if they are walking together along the road, however, physical affection (between a man and woman) is not openly displayed and is considered offensive. Greetings are very important. When greeting each other, people usually stand in a respectful attitude, sometimes bowing with hands clasped, enquiring about you and your health, your family, how you slept last night, your work, etc. and to which the response is always, "nzuri" or "salama" ("good" or "peaceful"). It is disrespectful not to observe this tradition.

My limited experience of Tanzania, where there are over 120 ethnic groups, is of a country of warm, friendly and peaceful people. During my stay in Dar, I did not feel unsafe or hassled, although once a man sidled up to me and asked, in perfect English, if I wanted to buy some Marijuana. I found this highly amusing. In some instances, there are petty thefts, however this is not widespread, as stealing is not condoned, and people are punished if caught, in most cases with severe beatings, sometimes even fatal. VSO cautions its volunteers about the consequences of shouting, "thief", "thief!". In-spite of grinding poverty, people are not 'grasping' and I never had the feeling anyone being 'nice' to get something from me. Rather, people are genuinely friendly, willing to walk alongside me, just chatting and very eager to help if I was struggling with the language. I left Dar on the 6th March (after one month in-country induction into language and customs training). I travelled by road to Dodoma, stayed overnight and continued the journey to Tabora by train, being due back in Dar on 10th June for a 2-day VSO conference, followed by two weeks Intermediate Kiswahili language training.

Tabora is an old town with an interesting history of Arab Slave-Trading. David Livingstone, the British explorer also lived here for a short time in 1871. It is far from being beautiful and is, for me, a physical and cultural desert island, isolated from other places because of poor roads. The train from Dar (850 km) passes through to Kigoma (a further 411km), 3 times a week. There are many positives however, for example a lack of tourists, and beautiful night skies. Mars is visibly red and Venus bold and dazzling. The African sky is spectacular with stars just lighting up the night.

Here, being novel and different, I am stared at, talked about and called names: Sister, Rasta, Mzungu, Teacher, Mama Edgar (this is how married women or those with children are addressed) or Mama Maendeleo (Mother of Development because of my work) Woman are also addressed by their husband's name or profession, so Mama Askofu is the Bishop's wife.

I find people's interest in me at times amusing, at other times tiresome. On seeing me approaching, market women crane their necks to get a better look. When it appears that I am about to buy something, they invite me with, "karibu, karibu" ("welcome, welcome"). My hair is the main

61

attraction, but a Black woman not being able to speak Swahili is peculiar. I have over-heard "Kiingereza" ("English", referring to me), in tones full of sympathy. One day, I was talking to an Anglican Priest, who said, "oh dear, what did you do that for?", when I told him I lived in England. Some people' experiences do not go beyond Tabora; some believe only white people live in England/Europe. So, when people call me 'Mzungu', they are calling me 'different', and I feel they are telling me that I am not one of them. I often meet people who know little or nothing about the Caribbean, so explaining where I was born is sometimes problematic.

Tabora Market is one of my favourite places. I love the buzz: the heady aromas, the colours, the shapes, evoking memories of the Caribbean: the fruit, the vegetables, the spices, reliving the remembered tastes and smells of my childhood. I love rummaging through 'mitumba': this is clothing donated by aid agencies: I have seen many clothes with tags from well-known Charity shops in England. This is a new line of business for women who sell the clothes from kangas spread out on the ground. I once found a brand new "Dickins & Jones" dress, which was just the ticket!

My most frightening experience in Tabora was being stoned. It happened as I passed the market early one morning. I took no notice of the stone which fell behind me, but when a second stone landed in front of me, I understood what was happening. I continued walking with a wildly pounding heart and a sound like a diesel locomotive in my ears.

In time I know this will all pass. I will be part of the rich fabric of Tabora and will pass unnoticed among all beautiful and precious things. I cannot wait for that time, for then I shall be able to do what I enjoy most, which is observing people. Till then I have no more than first impressions of Tabora, which, on the whole, are good and positive. I am told that Tabora is one of the best towns in Tanzania and over the next two years, I shall find out if that is so.

My home (a house first built for missionaries) is large and pleasant with modest facilities including an inside toilet. Thank God. I envisaged a pit latrine which filled me with horror. Having said that I shall not escape having to use pit-latrines when I begin working in the villages, and stay for up to a fortnight at a time. There is an electricity supply to the house, however, I am told that in the rain season, electricity is unreliable. I have been plunged into darkness on at least three occasions, which is scary. There is no water supply to the house, but fortunately there is a hand-pump well (the water is very salty) on the Compound. The distance between my house and the well is about 150 yards, so I do not have to carry water on my head like other women and children, some as young as three or four years. Here, girls begin to practise early for their burdensome life-tasks. Toilet-flushing in my home is manual and I am creative when taking baths. Water for cooking, drinking, teeth-brushing, washing fruit, vegetables and the dishes, must first, be thoroughly boiled and filtered. Healthy living depends on doing so.

It is strange living on my own and sometimes sleeping is difficult when I lie awake listening to sounds of the night. These are exciting. So far, I have identified birds, frogs, crickets, hedgehogs, but there are many sounds I do not recognise. I have a 12-foot snake (so I am told) as a neighbour. It lives in my garden under a large container (from America Overseas Aid), so I am very careful. After the initial shock of finding this out, I now feel a certain kind of protection from 'a snake in my backyard', with a fantasy that it will bite anyone who tries to get into my house through my bedroom window.

I am becoming 'domesticated' – I made curtains. This surprised me. I feel rather good about my new skills: the five large curtains I made from a beautiful African cloth. Though basic, they are my handiwork! It took time before I decided to use curtains, as I have never liked the 'shut-in-feel'. I did this after hearing noises outside in the blackness, two weeks after my arrival. I was left with the feeling of eyes looking in and watching me. Whether real or imagined, it inspired a poem, NIGHT IN TABORA.

Ann* (Nurse) and Robert* (Water Engineer) are VSO neighbours, who also arrived to work at the Moravian Development Office. We met for the first time in Dar. Their work is in Well-drilling and Sanitation. It is interesting to observe the dynamics when people meet us together. It can also be annoying and sad – for at best, some believe I am recipient rather than provider, because of ethnicity.

There is a largish white population in town: volunteers and missionaries from Europe and Japan, and tobacco farmers from South Africa. As the only Black volunteer, it gets difficult turning down offers to go out with this group of Volunteers, without seeming unfriendly. However, it is more important for me to spend as much time as possible in the company of local people where I can learn about customs, traditions and ways of African life. At other times, I like to spend in my creative mood and Writing.

I go to church on Sundays, despite not understanding much of the sermon. I hum familiar tunes or silently read hymns or use the 'time to be still'. I made a new friend, Adelyn. She is a Moravian missionary from St Kitts who has lived here for 15 years. She is now married with a Tanzanian family. We feel related as her grandparents are also from Nevis. Adelyn is a Nursing Sister at the Dispensary (part of the MCWT Outreach). She is called Mama Daktari (Woman Doctor) by her patients. She and the locally trained male doctor provide an excellent and much needed health service with very scarce resources. Being friends with Adelyn, helps relieve feelings of isolation: she is a great support and comfort to me.

I hope that from reading this first LETTER FROM TABORA, you will see glimpses of me in this harsh beauty. Thank you for allowing me to share my Journey with you and for your continuing good wishes and prayers. When nights are long they come to me. Thank you for being with me On The Road.

Amani (Peace) is sometimes said when parting.

I have changed their names

May 1997

I literally came Off The Road when the bus I was travelling on overturned. Physically, I was unhurt, apart from minor cuts, bruises and a jarring to my spine, but the effects were significantly serious for me to return home for treatment. VSO sent me to InterHealth, a home mission in Waterloo Road, which provides medical and psychological services for overseas aid workers.

The accident challenged my feeling of being 'in control of my own life' at a deep level and I was faced with a truth that tipped me over the edge. On my return home, my 'out-of-control' feelings manifested themselves in obsessive cleaning, a behaviour which is out of character, frightening and exhausting. Internalised anger found expression in me refusing to eat, and my weight dropped to under seven and a half stones. George patiently nursed me back to health. As a psychotherapist, I am interested in exploring my own links with Control, Food and now Tanzania.

I responded to these challenges with a feeling of outrage at being trapped inside the poverty of Tanzania: of being made vulnerable without 'on-the-spot' emergency services; of sitting in the shock of doing nothing – not screaming, not demanding, not protesting – just sitting in the 'will of God'. My anger was too frightening, too demanding and out of place in Tanzania, and I failed to understand why the local travellers did not express these (same) feelings. I felt trapped between inertia and carnage.

I was challenged too by the thought of dying far from my family in a country used to death and dying. Would they bury me within 24 hours, far from home, I wondered?

I was afraid, but I mobilised my thinking quickly: I was not dead the first time around, and I did not want to die in the second round from burning, trampling or suffocation, therefore I had to get out quickly. As I pulled myself from my up-turned position, I did not think of the danger of the bus continuing to roll, my need to escape being greater. My prayers were desperate, as I caught hold of a window and jumped out into a 'cassie' (acacia) tree. Ironically, for the first time I was wearing a skirt, as I learnt from an earlier safari (journey) that roadside toilet stops, on journeys taking seven, eight or more hours, do favour men.

I am now far removed from the Nightmare, although memories bring unreal thoughts that this is someone else's story. I still struggle with Faith and The Will of God and seem to be somehow stuck in my understanding or acceptance, caught between what I believe and the belief of many Christian people in Tanzania. My sense is that people here, express their personal disasters, for example losing a child or children through malaria; dying in childbirth; hunger and starvation; poor rains, droughts or other happenings as the "will of God". So, when a woman put her arms around my shaking body, telling me, "not to upset yourself so", because it was "the will of God", I go on searching to understand the meaning. What I am certain of is the overcrowded conditions on a poorly maintained bus, and questions remaining in my mind are related to 'need' and 'greed'. Gillian, my Christian sister, has given me a perspective: of a people with materially very little except a total faith and a belief in God, to sustain them. I learnt yet another view of faith and poverty from an English woman missionary with 17 years of work in

Tanzania, which is that maybe people "Let go and let God." My view is that "the will of God" as believed by Tanzanians carries a fatalism which is not in keeping with my own belief of exercising 'free will'. Maybe the reality of lives and experiences make questions of Faith complex.

My Faith is based on exercising personal choice and believe that somewhere in between different views is the Tanzanian Truth. I rather like Susan Taylor's thoughts in 'In The Spirit' (Andrea's farewell gift) where she writes that, "Having faith means being active, not sitting back bemoaning life and waiting for change to come". I take a philosophical view of HEBREWS 11: verse 1.

My reality is that I was able to walk away from that disaster while people who experience another reality just sat in their fate of being poor. Many may have spent the last money they had on the journey, only to lose all hope, but for me this was not my Sodom and Gomorrah. As a Black Woman, witnessing the meaning of this troubles me deeply. I can always escape, can always walk away, because I am just travelling through experiences such as these, as someone on the outside.

Back On The Road, I continue to wonder at the beauty of Tanzania and I am constantly reminded of how beautiful the country is, despite the scars of poverty. I feel blessed in experiencing Tanzania in such an intimate way, and although I sometimes get the feeling that people have little time to appreciate their country in the way I can, I feel it important to share with them the joy it brings to me. Everywhere the response is the same "Asante sana" (thank you), "Karibu" (welcome) and always with the feeling of 'welcome again' ("karibu tena"), which are memories that every visitor to Tanzania can take home.

George came out for a visit and we went to Tarangerie National Park, Lake Manyara and Ngorongoro, three of the country's finest national parks. For me, the Ngorongoro is how I envisage 'the First Eden'. Here one can feel in communion with all kinds of animals, just as God intended. I was spiritually moved and tried to capture some of The Ngorongoro on film, but how to capture the feeling? To photograph lions resting (even if they are in the shade of a Land Rover) feels like an intrusion into something sacred. A lasting memory is a pink horizon: flamingos on a crystal lake.

Mount Kilimanjaro from an aircraft, to me, is like a surrealist painting – a standing figure with feet loosely wrapped in fluffs of cotton wool and black eyes on top of a white head. Sunrise, as the plane approached Tanzania was so spectacular, that I can only describe it as a scene from Revelation. My words will fail to create the drama of mood and colour, but from a reading of Revelation you might get the feel of the Sun taking its time to come out of a sea of white feathery mountains and valleys, from layers of slowly changing patterns, to sit for a while on the clouds, on the edge of the world, like a magician's ball, dancing, and yet doing none of these things. Just observing a brilliance so pure it was not possible to gaze for more than a second. I hid my eyes and immediately hoped that I was not in "The Last Day", in which place I hope I shall not be hiding.

In my travels for work I am always 'discovering' new sights and meeting interesting and different ethnic groups:

The Wamaasai, Wasukuma and Watulu are traditional ethnic groups who still follow ancient traditions (in dress, language and customs).

When working in Igunga, 18th–30th April, a village without electricity, I saw an interesting looking 'star'. I later learned it was a comet. The night sky over Igunga was even more dramatic during those nights! Travelling to work in villages and towns, I shall see the wild beauty of Tanzania. Singida, on a plateau, has two soda lakes where flamingos from Lake Manarya visit and stay for a while. They had flown off when I arrived there the first time, but as I shall be working in this town, there will be other opportunities. My 'mystery star' giving a strange light was, I hear, causing great excitement in England, well at least in Croydon, so watching it here in Tanzania, makes me feel close to home. For the past nine nights since my return from safari, I fruitlessly hunted Tabora skies, until tonight, when I found it, looking pale and sad in the moonlight.

If you are wondering if this is a star-gazing holiday, full of excitement and only good things, that is hardly the case, the starkness of Tabora and work keep life real.

I live in Swahilini (so called by local people), a place where no one admits to living. Whenever I tell people where I live, some express sympathy. This is a part of Tabora, which, if fortunes were different and I had choice, I would escape, but then I would have suffered loss: not experiencing the fullness of Tabora; the variety, and, one which contrasts widely with my own. In this less than fashionable part of town, I am subjected to noise without escape. I have yet to discover interesting areas of Tabora with places to walk or hills to climb, or to find out that it is not all sand and despair without transport. Tabora is beautiful at night and pleasant evenings are spent sitting on my step improving my Kiswahili with Peter, a watchman (mlinzi) whose services I share with Ann and Robert.

Noise is a battleground on which I fight daily, and my complaints are grumpy obsessions with privacy. In truth, the noise level is no different to living in the heart of a bustling market town. The four mosques' call to prayer is 'kelele sana' (very noisy). Long 'political' and 'religious' speeches and canned music go on all night. The "speeches" are informative: sometimes a theft may have been reported to the Mosque and a warning is given on how stolen items can be returned without punishment. I do not know what the Christian/Muslim divide in Tanzania is, but one might be correct in thinking that it is 50/50. Some sounds from the Mosques are very pleasant and comforting, moving me to humming the tunes.

The Church on the compound praises God in loud voices and music: sometimes in most disagreeable sounds of competing choirs with electric guitars. My charitable feelings do not survive practice three times a week for many hours. The build-up to Easter was particularly tough: I was trapped in high-pitched nasal singing and the out-of-key electronic instruments, sent as Aid (from America). I was trapped in the disharmony. I longed to hear the African Drum taking up its honoured place in Christian worship. I still wait for these powerful vibrations on my eardrums! I escaped to the tranquillity of Lake

Tanganyika, and spent Easter in Kigoma, the lake-side town, to ponder God's tolerance for noise.

The Well on the compound is a bustling community meeting-place. When there are water problems in other parts of town, it seems as if all Tabora comes to The Well. There, life is lived out purposefully – people, including men, do the weekly washing, laying clothes on the ground to dry; children bathe and play; and men, sometimes, wash their bicycles there. For a few days, it was interesting to watch a group of women drawing water and going to and from a building site, using an organised system: while two women take turns in pumping water and filling buckets, other women use waiting times to sit and crochet. This 'system' continued until they finished working. This was one example of how well women work together in organised and harmonious groups. When there is a task to be done, like preparing for a celebration, the women come together for the planning and allocation of tasks.

So much of life is lived out at The Well, even going to toilet when they come to fetch water is quite common, and it is not only children who do this. Many times, I have watched with surprise, women just squatting down. I have noticed that 'going to toilet' is not a 'hide-away, private function'. I am learning how to "shut the eye" and not pass judgement on things and situations which are new to me. As I travel and work away from home, I often share table space with flies, cockroaches and other pesky creatures, eating in places that I would never have chosen. I do sometimes draw limits on what I am willing to accept, if I can get by without seeming rude or arrogant. One day, I went to the market to buy honey and the man serving me began pouring honey from one bottle to another bottle. He licked the over-pouring bottle to stop it from dripping, before offering it to me. Although Tabora Honey is famous, I found an excuse not to buy the honey!

I am learning so much about myself as I live and work here. I am becoming conscious of how easy it is to pass judgements and make comments about other people. I beg pardon now as I feel that, in the process of documenting my life over these two years, observations and judgements that I make, may be wrong and cause offence. I intend to write always with respect and hope that where I err, I shall be forgiven.

Tanzania has ancient cultures, rich in traditions and customs that still have links with biblical times. I feel this particularly when I observe certain rituals. There are significant rituals related to 'water' such as water which is for washing hands, water used for washing the dust from the feet, and water that is given to strangers to drink! There is also an uncomfortable sense of my 'not-belonging': when I feel that my 'Africanness' is still wandering in the Diaspora. Living here and realising how very much on the outside I really am, is a challenge I face every day. Every place I go to in Tanzania (because of my clothes, hairstyle and lack of Swahili) I am asked "Kabila Gani?", meaning what is your Tribe, and my reply is always "Sina" (I have none). In filling out forms, when asked for Tribe, I put British. This brings over me the feeling that I have been away from my 'Home/Africa', for a long time!

The Accident too was a turning point, and I concern myself less with worry, becoming more accepting of life. Two days after my return from England, I was riding on a

Dala-Dala in Dar. The only space available was standing close to the steps. I was wedged in by bodies! There was no space or place to hold on to, but I felt safe as long as there was no accident, when I would be thrown to my fate. I laughed to myself.

Minutes ago, I wrote about being accepting and tolerant, however, when 'trials of faith' appear, they come as ghosts of failed promises or frustrated expectations that change my thinking and I plummet to depths of uncertainty that ask, "what am I doing here?" In these times, I continue to look for signs and answers, instead of being strong in my purpose for being in Tanzania.

As Assistant to the Director, with special responsibility for the Small Scale Development Fund (SSDF), my title is Project and Development Officer. The Department lends money to Groups on a revolving basis, at a rate of 20% interest, and upholds the philosophy that micro-credit can make a difference to the very poor. It was encouraging to read reports from the first world summit on Micro-credit held recently in Washington, that the World Bank pledged support for Micro-Credit and the anti-poverty work.

In my experience of Micro-Credit, sometimes recipients cannot make repayments. This can impact negatively and sometimes hurt relationships. In one district where substantial sums of money are owed, 'debt-collecting' offers little scope for 'development' with people running away when they hear that I am visiting. I heard recently of one man who wanted to sell his house and run away with his two wives. This makes me sad. However, many people find success through the Scheme.

When faced with such levels of distress and hardship, it makes me realise the high price people pay for being poor. I feel that I am witnessing a poverty of dependency: a legacy of Christianity and other forms of colonisation. A Loan (from the Church) is perceived by many borrowers as a 'gift' and unconsciously creates a confusion in their minds. This is because giving and receiving 'gifts' is significant in Tanzanian culture, and the necessity to 'pay back' is not clearly understood, despite signed contracts. Many 'Borrowers' have little or no formal education and have limited skills in managing large sums of money.

Difficulties I face do not overshadow the overall satisfaction I have of working in a Christian organisation which is reaching out to the whole community. The MCWT* celebrated 100 years in December and continues to provide Health Services (9 Dispensaries and two Hospitals, one of which is a Leprosarium), Education Services – two secondary schools and Social Services through its Community Programmes. My neighbour Robert, the Water Engineer is digging wells in villages to make clean water accessible, which in turn improves health and alleviates the burden of women. His wife, Ann, a nurse by profession, is volunteering as a Health and Water Sanitation Officer, working with the villagers. In Usoke, a village 80 klm away, two other VSOs live and work in Education and Agro-Foresrtry.

I am responsible for The Heifer Project which is part of the Integrated Programme that helps people improve their economic situation. It follows the guidelines of Heifer Project International, whereby an in-calf cow is given free of charge to a farmer, who must first undergo training to prepare for receiving the animal by building a 'banda' (shed) and planting fodder for the animal to eat. This is the 'zero-grazing' approach, a disease control method of keeping cattle. The first and third female calves are given back to the Project, and will in turn, be given as a gift to two other farmers in the Scheme. After this contract is completed, the farmer owns the cow and has no further 'pay-back' commitment to the Scheme.

The MCWT Development Department is small but dynamic with a high profile in Tabora and its Provinces. I work with 4 men including the Director. I have an overview of the Department's work – I am currently writing the 1996 Annual Report, due at the end of the month. Writing proposals to Donor Agencies/Partners, is something I enjoy doing as this helps to sustain the Church's outreach.

I recently 'butted up' against the wrong side of Tanzanian Law and the Police for the offence of not giving 'right-of-way' to two women officers on a bicycle. The incident turned into a 'community bazaar' with people joining in to give advice. I was ordered by the officers into the station to stand in-front of a woman sergeant in a room full of unpleasant women officers. I experienced the discomfort of being questioned. They were nasty and resentful and could not understand how a Black person could come from England. My mind ran with thoughts which were unkind, uncharitable and full of stereotypes about 'the police'. I however humbled myself, said lots of "samahani", but was annoyed deep down. The man who was with me later told me that I was expected to give "a bribe." My fantasy was the distress of having my beautiful hair cut off and that I would have a shaved head in prison!

Racism is alive and kicking here in Tanzania. It transmuted in my mind with Disease, Antibiotics and Resistance. Men and women in domestic service are called, "house-boys" and "house-girls", who are "ever so good", or "ever so nice", but who never attain states of adulthood and respect. 'Change Agents' are here to ensure that Donors' money is protected from "incompetence" and "lack of structure", implications that Tanzania is unable to manage its own affairs. The obsession with, and the over-use of the word 'corruption', is very interesting, and would reveal much, if it were to be explored within an analytical framework! As the token Mzungu, I am expected to 'join in', to collude with many things said in my presence, which are offensive and are attacks on Tanzanian people. At these time, I too feel 'attacked'. Sometimes, I am unable to challenge racist views, assumptions and opinions as it may not be appropriate to do so at that time. These situations always leave me feeling angry and 'impotent'.

Last June, while attending a VSO Conference at the Bahari Beach Hotel in Dar, I experienced Racism in its crudest form. This luxury Hotel is beyond the means and experience of most Tanzanian people. One of my VSO male colleagues believing me to be a prostitute, quietly mentioned this to another male VSO. It did not matter to him that I was talking in the group or make sense to him that I was part of the group. When told that I was not a prostitute, but a VSO, he further implicated himself in his apology to me by stating that it was a "natural assumption to make because 99.9% of VSOs are White".

My interpretation is that as a Black Woman, being here was a challenge to his unconscious: Black people in places such as Bahari Beach Hotel are there to give services. That he felt safe and justified in saying this is revealing on many levels.

I value your prayers and letters. Thank you for joining me On The Road.

Amani (Peace).

July 1997

Kiswahili is an interesting language, with sounds, full of movement and music, and I am experimenting with it in poetry: "haya puzika, mungu akubarikie" ("OK, rest. God bless you") and "zima taa, wezi wengi sana nje", ("turn out the lights, there are many thieves outside") is full of rhythm and flavour. I hope translations of my Journey will release the rhythm and colours of Tanzania.

Sometimes I want to write about the 'not so good times', but shy away because I would hate for you to say, "oh dear" too often. Settling back in Tanzania was a struggle. For a long time, everything seemed to be going wrong. The Road is rough just now, but as I pass through the many 'mountains', the view is still beautiful.

My return to Tanzania, after recovering from the accident, was full of challenge and I almost missed my plane: George and I left home with enough time to negotiate the M25 on a Friday evening and while he parked the car, I had to hurry to the Gate, carrying what felt like my body weight as hand luggage. It was most unpleasant: bulging pockets; shoulders breaking with a motorcycle helmet and an over-stuffed bag, I felt my heart would burst. By the time I got into the plane. I was hallucinating with strain.

My sentiments were strangulating and worse, my Swiss Army knife was confiscated by Airport Security for safekeeping and lost. On arrival in Dar, my anger expressed itself in low mood.

The first months back were difficult: telephone calls from Tabora were unsuccessful and contacts were lost for about two months: letters did not arrive; I lost confidence and began obsessing about the welfare of my family. My colleagues were generous, especially when they knew I had been crying. Adelyn was an anchor during "these cut-off, roaming, wilderness days". My distress made me vulnerable to illness: I was unable to eat. In the first week in June, I suffered malaria and galloping tonsillitis with raging headaches.

As I recovered in bed, I read. Brian Keenan's, "An Evil Cradling" was excellent. I finished "An Entertaining Event" by Mary Wesley in one day. "The Remains of the Day", Kazuo Ishiguro, wrapped me in gentle humour. I got lively glimpses of East African cultures from Nicholas Proffitt's "Edge of Eden", set in Kenya, the Author takes liberties with Kiswahili, used words for effect rather than accuracy: a creative use of the language. However, a tendency to explain translations sometimes made the dialogue clumsy. I 'hiccupped' through uneven patches. I finished David Lodge's excellent "Therapy" having failed earlier to struggle through his madness! This book may be or may not be for 'hypochondriacs'!

Malaria is a dreadful illness. Treatments with quinine taste nasty, but 'Nasty Quinine' is a better gamble than 'Cerebral Malaria'. The 'shakes' is a frightening and lonely experience, but my many visitors made me feel I was in a Play: 'An Imaginary Malaria', about Tanzanian etiquette. I was inspired to write 'Malaria' to make sense of the 'rain in my head'. The poem took about five minutes to write, but then as always come 'days of ritual': grazing, dancing, chipping to shape in a never satisfied circle. The poem is now called "Quinine". The process was therapeutic. I feel recovered now, one month later, but weary.

A recent earthquake came with a frightening bang and a violent shaking of my world and I wanted to "run home". I looked up in the sky to see if this was the "Second Coming" and was relieved to find nothing changed. I imagine Gillian's warning to, "be ready and waiting in a state of grace". Life here seems more frightening since the accident and I yearn for the support and nearness of my family. Sadly, sometimes I feel love, support, family, friends, home remain in eclipse.

In a week or two a colleague in the office is travelling to Arusha for work and it seems too good an opportunity to miss, so I am using TOIL to take a welcome break, go to Arusha and buy Makonde Carvings. The finest of batiks are produced in Arusha. I recently bought three pieces when an Arusha-man came to the compound looking for the "Wazungu" (Robert, Ann and me). I was instantly taken with a 'Maasai Warriors' scene but unwilling to pay his asking price of TSh 25,000. I told him I was a volunteer without a wage. One is never expected to pay the asking price: bartering is acceptable. The "elfu Kumi, basi" (TSh 10,000 only), I offered was not fair, but, 'Arusha-Man' was willing to "win some and lose some", because, I was his "sister", but "don't let the other wazungu know". I bought two batik paintings and three woven baskets which cost me TSh 11,000. He was happy and left with no bad feelings. He had earlier made profitable sales to "Health Projects Abroad" Volunteers, (these are hard-working and committed young people who raise money to volunteer in Tanzania for up to 3 months. These young people contribute to positive development in rural areas, helping villagers to build their own dispensaries).

The outside world is still closed to much of Tanzania, and local people are genuinely surprised when they meet me, one expression is "Kumbe"! (Fancy That). Men up to a certain age in the Maasai tribe wear their hair in a style which resembles mine. So, my hairstyle puts me outside the status of a Maasai woman. I have, however, had many proposals of marriage. I am given labels: with price tags; and assumptions of 'The Other'. As a result, I forfeit many things as I refuse to pay exorbitant prices: like when I wanted to buy lobster at Kivukoni Market, the fisherman asked me for TSh 40,000. I am perceived as the Stranger - people expect 'gifts' (zawadi) from the stranger and cannot understand what it means to be a volunteer with little money. Many people come to my home to borrow money, which they are unable to repay. I soon learned that it is better to give food than money. So, these days, I have taken to buying 90 Kg sacks of maize grains and I share this out instead.

ESCAPE FROM NOISE is my book, in fantasy, that I shall write about living in Tabora. Writing 'the experience' may help me be more tolerant. For now, I plan escapes. It is important to plan escapes and I look forward to a week in Kigoma and the sanity of Lake Tanganyika when George visits. He too, will be glad of peace and rest, after the Tabora–Arusha bus safari which I have planned, and, the trip to Zanzibar, I know will soothe any painful bumps and bruises.

My bug for travel is spreading rapidly. Harare seems attractive. Maybe I shall find my long-lost friend, Pendeka!

It is possible to travel to Zimbabwe by bus: the cost of travel is cheap, but the journey is punishing.

Work feels in crisis. Since returning from safari at the end of April, I have been tied to office administration which is vital to the survival of the Organisation. This month work will suffer setbacks, however, life here is not rigidly bound by timetables. I am learning how to live and work within very flexible parameters, but I hope I shall be able to fit back into the home-market at the end of placement.

At a seminar for Church Women whose theme was 'The Family', I led a workshop which explored the concept of Group/The Family as a healing and forgiving place. In this part of Tanzania, the redundant style of group-work, where the teacher (Mwalimu)/group leader imparts all truth and knowledge and the participants are 'eager and unknowing and grateful to receive', is still used. I was astonished to learn that I was expected to 'teach' the Seminar in this way to about 30 women. I was however, able to encourage the women to share in the benefits of participatory learning.

Time spent with women, in groups etc, helped me to learn valuable insights into how Tanzanian women make decisions in their roles and responsibilities as wives and mothers, in providing for their families. The selflessness of their 'sister-hood' made me reflect on my own experiences as a working mother. I remembered telling myself that I mattered, and that giving presents to myself was not being selfish. My sisters never "choose" to treat themselves in their world, where 'choice' is an unthinkable luxury. As a feminist and witness to my sisters' experiences, I remain confused and unsure.

For a long while, I wanted to write about women. My failed attempts recognise that my sisters lead complex lives and it would be arrogant to be quick to write about lifestyles of which I know so little. I get glimpses into the labyrinth and feel that from time to time I hold some of the threads, and, still do not know the length, depth or breath of these lives. The Tanzanian woman is always giving. The little left to herself is hard and raw. God knows, I would surely fail as a Tanzanian woman.

To me these lives are part of the enigma of Africa and, in this river, there is fullness and beauty, even when it is dry. Tanzanian mothers always give without a grumble. What I have observed makes me believe that even babies think mothers are property. Once, whilst travelling on a bus I watched a baby playing with his blind mother's breast, which was left hanging outside her dress. This was so the breast was available, whenever he wanted it. I watched him drinking from it, and, at other times, squeezing it for his comfort or play. He had the breast all to his greedy self and I was choking on the resentment with an unhappy laugh inside me.

Babies do own the breast for two years and at the merest whimper, in goes the 'comforter'. They are carried on mothers' backs in kanga-pouches, leaving mothers free to work on farms, collect firewood, cook and sometimes to walk several kilometres to collect water, most times from the crack of dawn. From dawn to dusk, many Tanzanian women work for nearly 20 hours a day exposing themselves to fatigue. (Women Conference, July 1997, Dar es Salaam). Women contribute to the stability of the Nation by nurturing calm babies who are carried and fed whether mothers are sitting, walking, working or standing. One day I saw a forlorn naked breast just waiting 'outside' while the mother held her baby and chatted gaily with three other women, near Tabora Market.

My information on birth control is scant but I understand that there is a two-year abstinence gap between births. Alternate methods are not accessible to many woman and abortion is illegal. Women have little say over their bodies and reproductive cycles are controlled by husbands: the pill being thrown away by some. I witnessed a husband at a woman's health education seminar, who attended, instead of his wife. Women are raised to marry, bear children, please men and respect their husband's parent or they are not considered 'good wives.' A wife may be beaten and sent back to her family, who also sometimes beat her. If, for example, she is not a good cook, she goes home in disgrace. Painkillers are not available in childbirth, and the woman is discouraged from crying, as this brings bad luck. When a baby dies at birth or before baptism, the mother must not cry as this will bring bad luck and a failure to become pregnant again, and it is she (other times the man), who puts her dead baby in the ground without ceremony, as though she is sending the dead child back, to come back live in another pregnancy. I visited a mother whose baby died a few hours after birth. Although she welcomed me with a weak smile and without open signs of grief, her eyes were far away and sad. I grieved for this woman. I felt her pain.

In my bond with Tanzanian women, some sadness is possibly rooted in my trying too hard to blot out memories of my own 'play-house' learning and its feelings of trapped domesticity. Here, little girls do not play with dolls. At an early age, they are given responsibilities of caring for siblings. Toddlers are carried around skilfully lodged in young girls' jutting out hip bones, which serve as sitting places for the young child. Children begin school at 7 or 9 years old.

Most families depend on their farms (mashamba) for food. Women, in the main, work the land using a hoe. In some areas, the land is usually dry, lacking in nutrients and yields are poor. Tobacco farming is lucrative but exploits both the family and the environment. Men, in general, contribute little to farming until harvest-time when they are involved in the reaping.

Family life turns on the sharp edges of the weather: if the rains are late or do not fall, families are faced with starvation. This year, some parts of Tabora Region are in crisis.

Women work all their lives, beginning as very young girls, following their mothers to fetch and carry water. I watched a little girl no more than three years balancing a small bottle full of water on her head. She had filled the bottle at the well and walked home behind her mother. For me, this is not a novel experience, so when Dorothy, the woman who helps me at home, puts the basket on her head on market days, I recall painful childhood memories. It hurts to see women bending their backs or on their knees scrubbing floors. This convey a submissiveness that I find difficult to deal with. Here in Tanzania, I bear these hurts and uncomfortable feelings alone! It is not appropriate to talk about such things here as they have 'no translation'. Eating (in a traditional way), with hands, faces me with the class snobbery of my Caribbean childhood of 'etiquette and table-manners'.

Women carry the burden of families with few rights to their children who are usually the property of fathers and fathers' families. If a man 'drives away his wife', she must leave the children behind, except if the child is nursing; or if the man is not yet married to her, that is, where formalities have not yet taken place, such as the non-payment of the 'bride-price'. Until such time, any children are the responsibility of her father. Most women are emotionally and financially bound to men, their value being in their ability to serve and make men wealthy: to cook, bear many children and farm. Women have no share in the wealth and no say when one more wife is added to increase profit.

When a relationship ends (death; divorce), the woman may go to the next man, but must leave behind the children of her relationship. However, she is expected to raise any new children in her new family.

Traditions and customs are old and strong, and, for Christians, these are deeply rooted in the Old Testament. My understanding of the Muslim way of life is limited to two girls happily telling me they were sisters with the same father and different mothers. The marriage customs and traditions are different for Christians and Muslins. I learned about this when I attended a civil wedding ceremony (of a VSO colleague). The ceremony began with a question to the man: was he was Muslim or Christian. It seemed to us, the wedding guests, as a strange question. We all laughed, but it was not a joke. The Officer explained that it is custom to record the religion of the groom in the first ceremony, as a Muslim can marry four times and have 4 wives.

Life for Tanzanian men is "very hard", a man once joked. He told me that men walked every day to join friends to drink the local brew (pombe) and then returning home to eat and beat their wives. He said that men provide the maize, then they expect their food. A man is said to "have a kitchen" when he marries, however my experience is that men recognise and value the work women do. Men themselves work very hard, travelling long distances on bicycles in search of work as labourers, porters, night watch men, or machinists. More men than women are employed in jobs outside the home; in administration, in industry and as jobbing farmers. In towns and villages, men work as water-carriers, selling water from hand-carts to households and businesses. However, there are small businesses springing up for women, for example, the Sunflower Project, where women are engaged in the whole process: from planting seeds to harvesting of the oil.

In my work with women, I witness how eager some are to learn new skills and take on new projects so that they can help provide for their families. Some have even joined the Heifer Project, which is, in the main, for male farmers. They are making excellent progress. I have been involved in running workshops for up to a week at a time and women will travel long distances to attend sessions, bringing with them food to cook and any dependent children. Once they arrive at the venue, they organise themselves: to collect fire-wood, water, all their needs for a week away from home. One or two may be nursing babies, but that does not hinder them as there is no shame in suckling a child in public. My experience is that Tanzanian women are powerful, resourceful and hard-working. Their relationship with men is subtle, given that customs and traditions defer to men. It appears that this allows for a successful management of lives without open conflict. Women never present open and public challenges to men. The negative side of the man/woman relationship is that women in distress often suffer in silence. When a man asked me if I would come to live permanently in Tanzania, his feelings I feel sure were crushed by my answer.

Since writing about the 'two-year abstinence', I learn that in "grandmother's day, this was a period of grace, when she was sent back to the village to nurse her child. Grandfather meanwhile, took another wife," so the childbearing cycle was never broken. I do not know how the 'modern' family manage this as those were in days before Family Planning Programmes.

July 1st was a memorable day when I felt I had to get away quickly to be with 'ordinary people', for whom the only anxiety is where the next meal was coming from. Two hours into my journey to Arusha, over 410 km. from Tabora, I began to bitterly regret taking off without caring how I would manage this long journey by bus. Two hours more and I wanted the driver to put me off so that I could walk back home: Tanzanian roads go in straight lines and I was desperate, so felt I could find my way home. The agony in my body was making me scream inside. I was sitting in seat 49, which was over the rear wheels and the ride felt as though the bus was speeding over corrugated sand, my kidneys were being grated in a high-speed food processor. The bus later made a stop, I assumed for toilet, so I scrambled over heads, across the backs of seats and shared a tree with several women. I next saw the bus driving away (my bag and camera inside), I panicked and appealed lamely to people, no longer believing this was a 'toilet stop'. There was no evidence for this, with no houses in sight, but as people sometimes walk very long distances to find transport, I felt this was the only reason for the stop. To my relief, the stop was to mend the first of four punctures on the journey. Trudging through the heavy sand was like walking though deep snow. Getting increasingly dirty did not bother me. I was walking towards the bus!

The colours of sand are interesting: whitey-brown, brown-black, red, sometimes colours with no name. We travelled through colours of changing landscapes too and after several hours, my skin-colour too had changed into a rich ochre. Next to me sat a 'one-sided ginger-colour man': half of him: his head, hair, face, beard, eye-brow, eyelashes and clothes: was ginger-colour, covered dust. I had become interested in the colour of dirt under his fingernails and considered, ALL TRAVELERS HAVE DIRTY FINGERNAILS as an excellent book title. The bus was full of 'new people': 'new colours' of black people. I noticed a woman in the seat behind me, she was wearing a jet-black short wig, and, not the usual head-wrap. Wigs are big here, and, did she want to show it off! That too was

90

changing colours. I stifled laughs every time I looked into her face or looked at her head and saw her wig. This is the way I entertain myself on long journeys, by watching people and talking and laughing to myself.

I thought it expedient to make friends with the woman for the next 35 hours (including statutory breaks and 'puncture stops'), as it made me feel we were sharing in a common discomfort. This was 'my fantasy', for when I tried to say how 'the stops' favoured men, she just stared, signalling no support for that idea. I felt the woman either could not understand my poor Swahili or was too tired to engage in my subversion. More men than women speak English, which indicates opportunities for education. Customarily, travel is in long silences – men and women do not engage in conversations. An advantage of me being a 'mzungu' is the freedom to talk freely with men, so long journeys are punctuated with chats in English.

I talk about 'going to toilet' freely and do not feel embarrassed. It is one of my survival strategies for long journeys. Me 'needing the toilet' on long journeys carries potential for either relief or dashed hopes and the silent anxiety of whether I will scramble over seats, barge past in good time, is an ever-present part of long journeys. Barging is in order. Travelling without a common language triggers my creative mind and the skill of watching people: for this purpose, I watch women. At one of the 'stops', I saw women were getting off and I was late 'barging through'. The men were already standing in lines relieving themselves as I ran through their lines, repeating "Sorry. Sorry", forgetting to say, "Samahani". At night, when it is unsafe to go in the bush, because of snakes, etc, we women just squat behind the bus. This is no problem, men and women mutually respect each other. Women's safety and privacy are never violated.

That night, we pulled up by the side of the road to sleep. I slept on my hands. The first job for the driver and crew next morning was to mend our fourth and final puncture. Most of the passengers cleaned up and used a nearby latrine. I crept into a convenient shamba: I could not face a pit-latrine, on an 'early-morning stomach'. A cockerel and his hens, in a basket on top the bus began welcoming the day.

I am becoming 'well-travelled and seasoned with experiences', such as fowls with their bottoms in plastic bags. In-spite of so much life and movement, I feel that I travel alone, 'without words' and I am always watching other people for clues, learning what to do, what the rules are. On these long-distance travels, there are many animals travelling on the roof of buses: chickens in cages, goats tethered and bleating, foam mattresses, hand-made wooden bed-frames, and other household items. On the journey home, I sat beside a fowl which was carried by a girl, holding his feet and tail feathers in a plastic bag. We had been travelling for hours in hot sun, that was getting hotter and hotter as the hours went slowly by and with only a hot wind blowing through glassless windows to tame the smell.

I laugh a lot in Tanzania, where sometimes even serious situations present comic sides. Soldiers, many of whom wear heavy, over-sized boots that emphasize scrawny legs; the Tea-seller walking along Dodoma Station platform with a coal-pot on her head boiling tea, evoked memories of a Caribbean childhood and made me laugh; a ragged-trousered boy dragging his reluctant feet in the sand as he led an old blind man, they were both holding either end of a long pole. He was wearing the most inappropriate tacky 'charity' sunglasses. In my mind, poverty and comedy are related, but I cannot explain what I mean by stating this. Life is lived out in so many bizarre ways. Even the cock on the bus roof is sensitive of his situation: he knows he is on his way to the cooking pot, however his pride and responsibility were not bound by his circumstance. He too is living in the moment!

On the way to Arusha, one of the challenges is Sekenke Mountain pass and our instincts responded well to the fascination with danger. Passengers stood up to look down with wonder into where we might end up. I watched the driver, who was constantly watching the performance of his slow-leaking tyre. My worry was for approaching lorries. After we had cleared the most treacherous, meandering section and were still climbing, we came upon an overturned lorry blocking the road. The forest on either side only just afforded our driver space to pass the accident, which he did without stopping. A man noticed me, hiding with panic under the seat. He said, "madam, we walk with death". His voice echoed the fatalism which is unshakeable throughout Christian and Muslim Tanzania. His words were my nightmare, again. As our bus climbed slowly up the steep mountain road, news filtered through that the driver of the overturned lorry had received a broken arm. His mate also escaped serious injury and was busy putting tree branches on the road. This is an 'agreed warning sign' amongst drivers that there is a road accident. Sekenke has little margin for error, and is unforgiving!

On the way back to Tabora, we descended Sekenke by inches and in God's hands, at 2 am in the morning. Outside our bus, except for engine sounds and headlights, the silence of the night was as total as the darkness. My seating companions were a teenage boy and his female relative. He slept for most of the way, on my back when my head was on my knees, on my shoulder or on his relative.

Earlier, I spoke little to this talkative woman, which fired her curiosity into gossiping about me with a man. I gave him a 'cut-eye', which was a message for both of them. This overly anxious woman did not want to bear her own fear alone. As we approached the mountain road, she woke the boy up with the hysteria of "SEKENKE" in her voice. I breathed out "Nashukuru Mungu", as if it was appropriate to thank God in Swahili, when we descended the mountain without crashing. Addressing no one in particular, the woman asked loudly if we had reached the bottom. I answered her, not because I felt kindly towards her, but because it helped to share the relief of coming out alive from potential disaster, by talking to another person.

Arusha Region is strikingly beautiful with mountain ranges and the impressive Ngorongoro Crater. Lake Manyara is visible from the road, but too far away for animals to be seen. En route, we could see zebras, ostriches, baboons, camels (imported for Camel Safaris). I recalled last year when George and I visited the National Parks, our vehicle made at least two stops for zebra (s) crossing the road. True!

I stayed at the YMCA which was cheap and clean. This is not the place to stay if one wishes to have privacy: plasterboard partitions only go half way to the ceiling and even gently snoring sounds are very loud. "Touts" or "Flies" walk up and down outside hotels and other places where guests stay, seeking opportunities for contacts. The city is full of souvenir sellers, newspaper men who hold their paper with style, batik sellers who never tire of undoing 'their roll' and the "Half-a-Sandwich Board Men" who carry a cacophony of items, all in plastic, pinned in orderly rows. Almost anything is available, even a Rolex watch, in plastic!

My tonsillitis was back and angry and for two nights I tried to stifle the irritating cough with my face in the mattress. From my 'room with a view', I could see the Equator Hotel where George and I stayed last year. Staying there instead of at the YMCA would have been 'just the ticket', but TSh 6,000 a night was more affordable than the TSh 18,000, I would have had to pay, even at 'residents rate'.

For three days it rained, and I was ill prepared for what was like a late spring day. My toes turned purple with cold. I stayed in bed and read "Child Bride" by Wang Ying, an interesting book on women in feudal China. From time to time, I gazed from the window. On other days, I walked around this lovely part of the town, separated by River Naura. Arusha is part of Tanzania's 'tourist circuit' and is always busy and full of people looking for safari trips to the National Parks, or a Mt Kilimanjaro Climb, before they move on to Dar and Zanzibar. I loved the 'movement'!

I also enjoyed hours sitting alone in the heart of River Temi, the water flowing, at this time of the year, was very low and in no big hurry, and as if picking up my mood. I felt the beauty of Tanzania wrapped round me: Mt. Meru from its lofty heights; sounds of river-water tumbling over rocks and in some places, seeping out like a stain in the ground. I rested my feet in the water and watched people in the distance crossing to their homes on the other side.

The 'Lonely Planet' states that The National Museum "must be a joke" and I understood the meaning when I visited. There is hardly anything to look at, however, Arusha is not harmed by this. It remains an important 'tourist town'.

I was delighted to be able to say, "siyo mtalii, ninakaa hapa, Tabora" ("I am not a tourist, I live here, in Tabora"), when people mistook me for a 'tourist', especially to the Maasai craftswomen, whom George and I had met last year. Now they were calling me 'shoga' (woman-friend). I was pleased. This also meant that I was able to buy their lovely beaded jewellery for small prices. These women's business-English, despite no formal education, is impressive. During my stay, I met three Wamaasai men who had been to university. Two were researching Tourism and its effects on Indigenous Peoples. Both thought VSO was doing useful work in their country.

The Wamaasai people never stay away long from their communities and so manage to bridge the gap with the outside world without compromising culture, despite threats from tourism. (I was disappointed last year to see traditionally dressed women on the 'Ngorongoro Rim' crying "Picha Picha", i.e. needing to beg). I enjoyed the Tanzania spirit of hospitality in Arusha for 10 days.

The planned return to Tabora with my colleague was unsuccessful due to YMCA policy on safeguarding guests' privacy. We were unable to make contact and I returned to Tabora by bus. The top of the bus was stacked dangerously high with cargo, including live animals and fowl: the traffic police gesticulated wildly; people stared, open-mouthed; drivers shook their heads and I interpreted the horror on their faces as a sign that the bus would overturn.

Overhead electric wires were sparking from the load on the bus top touching overhead live cables. Neither Driver nor Crew seemed worried. As the bus drove through the town, the Crew got off and guided the driver through the overhead electricity with shouts of: "ACHA". "NGOJA". "POLE-POLE". "NENDA". ("STOP". "WAIT". "SLOWLY". "GO"). I could see the overhead power-lines from my seat and as the bus approached each one, my head would dive to my knees and I would push fingers hard in my ears and wait for Death. In my mind I read: "PASSENGERS ELECTROCUTED", "BURNED ALIVE". Fear was like a vice squeezing life out of me. I felt like I was being tortured. Our driver drove on for 26 hours, ignoring the 10pm–4 am break, when buses, lorries, oil-tankers etc. are required by law to stop driving. This is part of the government 'Fatalities Prevention' strategy—an attempt to address the horrendous number of road fatalities. Our driver took no notice of this.

Passengers are silent hostages to the perils of travelling in Tanzania, because choice is poor or not available. So, for example, there were no protests when, at midnight, we pulled into a petrol station in Singida and our driver walked around smoking a cigarette as the tank was being filled. And so, 'the dance with death' continues and the floor space seems smaller each time the music stops!

I said goodbye to Ann and Robert and as the Tabora to Dar es Salaam train pulled away, 'things' came flying out: a sack full of chickens, a sack of rice which burst on impact, a sack of maize and a man, who jumped off the train. I stuffed two escaping chickens back in the sack and watched the crowd gather round the man who was scraping up dirt with the rice that had fallen out of the sack. I set about imagining why he decided to throw himself and his goods off the train at that time. Maybe he was asleep on the train which had travelled overnight from Kigoma, or he forgot something, maybe his ticket, and decided to throw himself off before the Guard did. The disaster last May when M V Bukoba - a Lake Victoria Ferry - sank, killing up to a thousand people, has had an impact on Public Travel and Safety. Somewhere in there could be the reason for this man's actions.

It is good to talk about what feels like a 'see-saw journey' through Tanzania. Thank you for staying with me On The Road.

Amani.

With George in Tanzania: Funerals and Other Ceremonies.

George came out twice for visits during which we travelled around going to wild-life parks including Tarangerie National Park, Lake Manyara and Ngorongoro, and enjoying days together in the vibrant towns and cities. On both his visits to Tanzania, George attended a funeral. As he was the only white person, he really stood out.

I watched him in this unique situation: sitting on the floor with the men (men and women sit separately) and using his hands to eat from a communal plate. It made me happy to see how well he behaved at these ceremonies, observing customs and tradition. He felt awkward though and later asked me, "is it necessary to arrange a funeral every time I visit?"

"The guest is king". This is an important part of Tanzanian culture. When George and I visited Kigoma, he experienced the meaning. Here, he was a guest at a wedding and the only white person in the church. He sat respectfully throughout the long ceremony, understanding only with his eyes. Neither he nor I can recall an invitation: we were just on holiday. We knew no one, however word got around that guests had come to town. So George was a 'guest' at this joyful celebration.

Later we travelled to Ujiji, 6 km from Kigoma, to visit the David Livingstone Memorial Museum. The highlight of that visit was the 'talk' given by Mzee, the museum guide. George and I were the only visitors on that day. After seeing The Exhibition – consisting almost solely of two elongated papier mache figures of David Livingstone and Henry Morton Stanley greeting each other – we sat under a mango tree and listened to Mzee deliver his Speech.

He stood before us, hands clasped to his chest and rattled off the history in a high-pitched voice and speed which was mechanical, rote-like and in an almost Victorian style of "teaching and learning." Both of us were careful not to be rude, holding our heads down and stifling laughs until he drew in his breath, signalling the end. After we paid Mzee, he begged George for a share of his lunch.

Later, as we walked round Ujiji Market enjoying the colours, shapes and smells, a naked man, covered in nothing but dust, ran up to George, shaking a dried-up snake. We were terrified at first, wondering if he held a sword. We were relieved to see what he was holding and to find out he was harmless. A laughing crowd gathered round us, giving their opinions.

George was lucky to get a front seat in the Dala-Dala, on our way back to Kigoma. He had earlier endured a very painful journey on the way to Ujiji, bent double on an over-crowded bus.

Towards the end of our week stay in Kigoma, we visited six Chimpanzees at their 'peninsular home on Lake Tanganyika'. This is a Jane Goodall Project set up for rescued chimpanzees who were stolen as babies from the wild, and, sold on to be smuggled out of the country. There is a market for baby chimpanzees, as wealthy people in other countries want to keep them as pets. These chimpanzees were intercepted at Dar es Salaam Airport.

One jealous male, now grown up, became angry that George was talking with his female carer and stoned him with large rocks, aiming these over high-wire fencing with amazing accuracy.

What George brought home from his visits to Tanzania was the 'welcome' and hospitality he was shown by all with whom he came into contact. He recalls visiting a Tanzanian home and, when he thanked the woman for receiving him, he remembers her telling him, "when we welcome a stranger into our home, we do not know, but we could be welcoming an angel."

Reference

English Translations of Kiswahili Words

C	chai	tea
	chai mzewa	tea with milk
	chai rangi	tea without milk
D	degaa	tiny fish about 5 cm long
	degedege	convulsion
G	gari	car/any motor vehicle
H	hakuna matata	there is no problem (no problem)
	house-boy/girl	a particularly demeaning name given to domestic workers, inspite of a person's age
I	inshallah	God willing
J	jambo	hello
	Jeshi la Wokovu	Salvation Army
K	karibu	welcome
	kanga	garment worn by women in East Africa, and sometimes by men
	kuja	come, come here
	kwaheri	goodbye
M	mama	how all married women are addressed
	maziwa	milk
	maduka	shops
	mchawi	witch (wachawi - witches)
	mlinzi	watchman
	mzungu	white person

	mzee	how an old man is addressed, a title of respect
N	ngoma	drum
	ngriti	warthog
	nzuri	good
P	pole	condolences
	pikipiki	motorcycle
S	saidia	help
	salama	safe or secure
	samahani	sorry
	safari njema	journey/have a good journey
	shilingi	TSh Tanzanian Shillings
	shamba	field
	shetani	the devil
	sindikiza	walking a visiting guest part of the way, when saying goodbye
T	tuonane kesho	see you tomorrow
U	ugali	a staple diet, made from maize flour
	uso mbaya	ugly face

Towns and unfamiliar place-names

- Arusha – in northern Tanzania, and the site of the Arusha Declaration 1967, known as Tanzania's most prominent political statement of African Socialism, 'Ujamaa', or brotherhood.
- Dar - Dar es Salaam - Capital of Tanzania
- Dodoma - Administrative Capital of Tanzania. Seat of Houses of Parliament. 583.64 km from Dar
- Kigoma – a large town on the eastern shores of Lake Tanganyika
- Lake Nyasa is also called Lake of Stars. This is because of the lanterns against the night sky. I have watched this and it is a magnificent sight.
- Morogoro - Produces fruit including pineapples, mangoes, bananas, pawpaw. 196 km from Dar.
- Matema Beach is on Lake Nyasa
- Saa Nane is an 0.76sq km island of mountain stones in Lake Victoria
- Tabora, 850 km west of Dar and 411 km east of Kigoma

Irma Upex-Huggins – Biography

Irma refers to herself as a 'words sculptor'. She is a retired Mental Health Social Worker and Group Analytic Psychotherapist. She lives in Croydon with her husband and dog, Kiki. She describes herself as an 'inquisitive observer of people, looking in from outside'. She enjoys travelling: loves the intimacy of small places: island communities, small towns, always visiting markets on her travels and learning about people, lives, languages, customs. She is the author of two other poetry books: *Aloes and Brown Sugar* (1991) and *Charcoal Woman* (1993). Irma is a member of Poets Anonymous. She plays guitar.

VSO – Voluntary Service Overseas

The poems and prose in "Red Winds" were written as a result of the period Irma Upex-Huggins spent as a VSO volunteer in Tanzania. She has decided to donate all her proceeds from sales of the book to Voluntary Service Overseas in Tanzania – to support their work with women.

While Voluntary Service Overseas is not responsible for the content of the book, they have said they will be most grateful for any donations made to their mission. Anyone wishing to know more about Voluntary Service Overseas, or to help in their work can reach them at https://www.vsointernational.org/

The charity's Registered Office Address is 100 London Road, Kingston upon Thames, Surrey KT2 6TN, and their Registered Charity number is Charity Registration 313757 (England and Wales) SCO39117 (Scotland).

Palewell Press

Palewell Press is an independent publisher handling poetry, fiction and non-fiction with a focus on Justice, Equality and Sustainability. The Editor may be reached via enquiries@palewellpress.co.uk

www.ingramcontent.com/pod-product-compliance
Lightning Source LLC
Chambersburg PA
CBHW050736030426
42336CB00012B/1602